W9-AJP-396

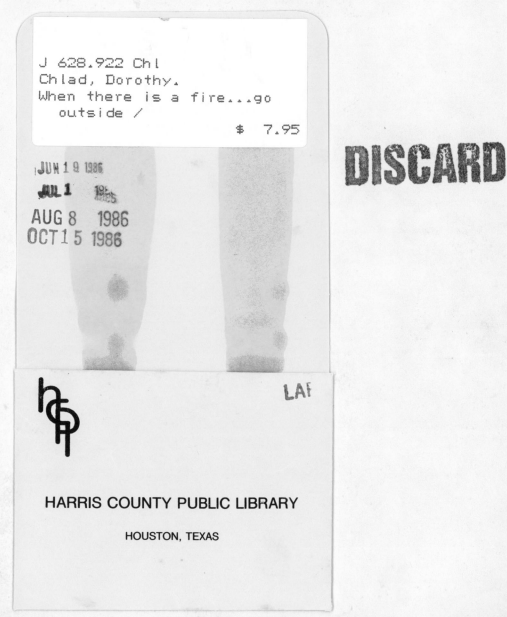

DISCARD

LAF

When There Is a Fire... Go Outside

By Dorothy Chlad

Illustrations by Lydia Halverson

 CHILDRENS PRESS, CHICAGO

Library of Congress Cataloging in Publication Data

Chlad, Dorothy.
    When there is a fire—go outside.

    (Safety Town)
    Summary: Presents safety rules to be
followed in case of a fire in the house.
    1.   Fire prevention—Juvenile literature.
2.   Fire extinction—Juvenile literature.
[1.   Fire prevention.   2.   Fire extinction.
3.   Safety]   I.   Halverson, Lydia, ill.
II.   Title.   III.   Series: Chlad, Dorothy.
Safety Town.
TH9148.C46   628.9'22   81-18108
ISBN O-516-O1986-4   AACR2

Hi. . . my name is Tony.

I want to tell you
what to do if there
is a fire.

At our house, we have plans. There are many different types of fires. So we have different ways to get out of the house. We practice our plans often. We know what to do if there is a fire.

We have smoke
detectors at our
house. They tell
us if there is too
much smoke or a
fire at our house.

8

We have fire
extinguishers at
our house, too. We
use them if there
is a small fire.

I am going to
tell you some of
our fire rules.
When there is a
fire, go outside.
Move quickly, but
do not run or push.

Never hide in a closet...

or under the bed.

Call the fire
department from
the house next door.

Tell the fire
fighters where the
fire is. They must
know the number of
the house and the
name of the street.

The fire fighters
will get on their
fire truck. They
will put on their
lights and sirens.

Now people can see
and hear them.
They know the fire
fighters are in a
hurry to help someone.

My friends and I
never go near the
street or run after
the fire truck. We
could get hurt.
And the fire fighters
would not get to
the fire as quickly
as they should.

Sometimes the
fire fighters use
their ladders.
They help get people
out of the house
or building. Then
they will put out
the fire.

When a fire is small,
a fire extinguisher
can be used.

When a fire is large,
hoses are used.

A fire can happen
anytime. . . .anywhere.

I hope your family
has a fire plan.
Then if there is
a fire in your house,
you will know
what to do.

My friends and I
hope you will remember
our fire safety rules:

1. When there is a fire, go outside.

2. Go quickly, but do not run or push.

3. Never go back into the house or building when it is burning.

4. Go to a neighbor to call the fire department.

5. Never run after the fire truck.

About the Author

Dorothy Chlad, founder of the total concept of Safety Town, is recognized internationally as a leader in Preschool/Early Childhood Safety Education. She has authored six books on the program, and has conducted the only workshops dedicated to the concept. Under Mrs. Chlad's direction, the National Safety Town Center was founded to promote the program through community involvement.

She has presented the importance of safety education at local, state, and national safety and education conferences, such as National Community Education Association, National Safety Council, and the American Driver and Traffic Safety Education Association. She serves as a member of several national committees, such as the Highway Traffic Safety Division and the Educational Resources Division of National Safety Council. Chlad was an active participant at the Sixth International Conference on Safety Education.

Dorothy Chlad continues to serve as a consultant for State Departments of Safety and Education. She has also consulted for the TV program "Sesame Street" and recently wrote this series of safety books for Childrens Press.

A participant of White House Conferences on safety, Dorothy Chlad has received numerous honors and awards including National Volunteer Activist and YMCA Career Woman of Achievement.

About the Artist

Lydia Halverson was born Lydia Geretti in midtown Manhattan. When she was two, her parents left New York and moved to Italy. Four years later her family returned to the United States and settled in the Chicago Area. Lydia attended the University of Illinois, graduating with a degree in fine arts. She worked as a graphic designer for many years before finally concentrating on book illustration.

Lydia lives with her husband and two cats in a suburb of Chicago and is active in several environmental organizations.